MW01001608

A Way of Life
for Young Catholics

by
Fr. Stephen Wang

*All booklets are published thanks to the
generous support of the members of the
Catholic Truth Society*

Contents

- Using this Book -

This Way of Life is written for young Catholics who
want to live their faith more deeply but are not sure what
steps to take. It contains practical, down-to-earth advice
on all sorts of issues that come up in the lives of young
Catholics. It is not for experts, but for ordinary young
people who have been touched by God in some way but
are not sure how to respond. It will be especially helpful
for older confirmation candidates, for students at college
and university, and for young adults who are hoping to
learn more about their faith and put it into practice in the
reality of their daily lives.

This is not the kind of book that you read straight
through. It is designed so that you can dip into it. Look
at the "Table of Contents" and see if anything interests
you. There are lots of lists and headings and things to do
- this is to make the book clear and easy to use. The risk
with giving lists is that we become overwhelmed and do
nothing, and end up feeling guilty about what we haven't
done! But the ideas that follow in this *Way of Life* are
not meant to be a burden. They are here to give you food
for thought, to guide you if you are stuck, to put you in
touch with the wisdom and experience of the Church, and
hopefully to inspire you. Perhaps one or two suggestions
will strike you, and you will be able to put them into
practice. You could keep this *Way of Life* on your desk

or by your bed, and come back to it now and then. See if something new strikes you. As you grow in the spiritual life, the Lord will give you new insights just when you need them. And he will nudge you to take new steps when the time is right.

I would like to thank the following people who looked at earlier versions of the text and offered invaluable suggestions about how to improve it: Robbie Low, Kate Finnegan, Simon Bishop, Katy Whisenant, Clare Watkins, and Fergal Martin.

- How to Live your Catholic Faith -

FIVE ESSENTIALS OF CATHOLIC LIFE

Whatever is happening in your life, however busy you are, however lost you feel - these five essentials are the foundation of the Christian life. Do everything you can to make them a part of your life.

1. Daily Prayer - In prayer, we lift our hearts to God, and we let him enter our lives. We don't need to pray a lot, but we do need to pray every day. If we don't, then our faith gets weaker and our love grows cold. At the very least, we can give two or three minutes at the beginning of the day when we wake up, and at the end of the day when we go to bed. It costs us nothing - but what a difference it makes! In the morning, for example, we can pray the Morning Offering, and say the Our Father, and ask God to bless our day. In the evening, we can thank God for the blessings of the day, and say sorry for our sins by saying an Act of Contrition, and finish with the Hail Mary and the Glory Be. These prayers are the foundations of our faith.

2. Sunday Mass - Whenever we go to Mass, the Lord speaks to us through his Holy Word; we are united with Jesus in the Sacrifice he offered on the Cross for our salvation; we meet him in Holy Communion; we receive the power of his Holy Spirit; and we are united with the whole Church across time and space. It is the holiest act of worship possible on earth. Sometimes we feel inspired, sometimes we feel a bit dry; sometimes we feel very peaceful, sometimes we are completely distracted. The important thing is that we are there, every Sunday. This is not so much a duty, as an invitation. The Lord is there for us. He asks us to love and honour him, and invites us to share his life. How can we refuse? Whatever is happening in your life, however difficult or dry things are - do everything you can to be at Sunday Mass. Don't pretend it doesn't matter, or you are too busy. (We are not obliged to go to Sunday Mass if we are too sick to go, or if we are looking after someone who needs our care and we cannot get away, or if we are travelling and unable to find a church for Mass).

3. Regular Confession - In the Sacrament of Confession, Jesus forgives us our sins, pours out his loving mercy upon us, begins to heal what has gone wrong in the past, and helps us to make a new start in our lives. Of course we can say sorry to God at any time - but there is no more powerful way of receiving God's forgiveness than by going to a priest for confession. And if we have committed any serious sins ('mortal' sins), then we need to go to confession to receive absolution so that we can receive Holy Communion again.

Confession should be a regular part of our lives. A good habit is to try and go every month. We might end up saying the same things each time, or even feel that we don't have much to say - but gradually this habit will help us to grow in holiness and grow closer to Christ. Don't worry if you haven't been to confession for ages; don't worry if you are shy or embarrassed. The priest will help you. (See the section 'How to go to confession' p. 47).

4. Keep the Commandments - It matters how we live our lives. We are called to love God and to love our neighbour. We are called to be holy. Everyone is different, but there are certain ways of life that will help us to be holy, and other ways of life that take us in the wrong direction. We don't have to make things up as we go along: God has revealed to us the way to holiness, in the Ten Commandments, in the teaching of Jesus, and above all in the life and death of Jesus himself, as he lays down his life for us in love and service. And still today, God guides us in our Christian lives and in our moral decisions through the teaching of the Catholic Church. We may struggle and fail in our moral lives, but we can all make a fundamental decision to turn away from evil and to try and live a good life. This decision is what matters most, because then God can help us - in his own time - to overcome our weaknesses and grow in holiness. We can renounce sin, and promise to do everything in our power to keep his commandments.

5. Love Your Neighbour - Your neighbour is whoever you are with at any moment. It might be someone at home, or at work, or at college; it might be someone in the street or in the shop; it might be someone you are phoning or emailing or instant messaging. You might be very close to this person, or you might not know them at all. Whoever they are, you are called to love them, to be kind to them, to respect them, to support them, and to pray for them. It may be that we cannot do much to help them at this time. And it is perfectly natural and good that we should care more about those we are close to (family, relatives, friends, etc.) than about those we hardly know. But the essential thing, once again, is simply to make a decision that we will try to love our neighbour. We are bound to fail sometimes, and there will be situations where we have no idea why or how we should love someone. But at least we know that this person is my neighbour, and they deserve my love, and we will not pretend that they don't exist or that they don't matter.

FIVE ACTIVITIES THAT WILL HELP YOUR FAITH

We can't do all of this, all at once. But here are some things that can help us in our faith. See what is possible for you, and what is helpful. Take a risk - try something. And if it helps you to be stronger and happier and holier in your faith, then that is probably a sign that you should keep it up!

1. Visit the Blessed Sacrament - Some Catholic churches remain locked all day; but many, thank God, are still open. Jesus Christ is present in the Blessed Sacrament, reserved in the tabernacle. This is not just a metaphor or a symbol. He is truly present, true God and true man, in all his power and glory and majesty. Whenever we come near to the tabernacle, even if the Blessed Sacrament is not exposed, we come into his hidden but powerful presence; heaven is laid open before us; and we can share our lives with him in a most intimate and profound way. If you can, make some time to pray before the Blessed Sacrament each week. Make a special 'visit' to the church, just for a few minutes. Or set aside some time before or after Mass for this purpose.

2. Go to Weekday Mass sometimes - You already go to Mass on Sundays, and that is the most important commitment. If there is time in your routine, try and go to Mass during the week; perhaps once a week, or once a month. There might be a Mass at your home church in the early morning or evening; or a lunchtime Mass near your college or work. This 'extra' Mass, which will be quieter and shorter than the Sunday Mass, is another way of dedicating our life to the Lord, and letting his love touch the ordinariness of the week. The power of his Word, and of Holy Communion, give us extra strength and guidance for our daily lives.

3. Do some Spiritual Reading - Find a Catholic spiritual book that encourages or inspires you in your faith. It might be about prayer, or the Christian life, or the saints, or Catholic belief. It doesn't matter, as long as it helps you. And read a little bit each day; or each week (perhaps on a Sunday). It is amazing how much a few wise thoughts can help us. We realise we are not alone. We learn new and exciting truths. We go deeper. Faith is the greatest adventure; and there are many inspiring people there to help us.

4. Join a Catholic Group - As young Catholics, it is good to get involved in parish life somehow. There are usually many things happening. If there doesn't seem to be much, be brave, and get together with some friends and suggest something that you could do as a parish to your priest. It also makes such a difference if we can find a Catholic group to join, with like-minded people. It helps us to feel that we are not alone in our faith. It might be a prayer group, or a justice and peace group, or a pro-life group, or a discussion group, or just a socialising group - all that matters is that there are Catholics trying to live their faith together in some way. Look around and see what there is, and then take the risk of joining one. If it works out, fine. If not, then don't give up - try another. You may have to look outside your parish and travel a bit. But it will be worth it. (There is a list of some groups and movements at the end of this book).

5. Go on Retreat or Pilgrimage - There are many kinds of retreats, prayer festivals, away days, pilgrimages, etc. Some of them might be organised by your parish or Diocese, others might be on a national level. It is good to get away from our daily routine now and then, with other Catholics, and focus on the Lord and on our faith. Not every retreat or pilgrimage will suit you personally, but you should be able to find something that is right for you. Ask your parish priest; look in the Catholic newspapers; ask some of the Catholic groups and movements listed below.

FIVE WAYS TO APPRECIATE THE MASS MORE

1. Learn about the Mass - Find out more about the meaning of the Mass by reading, or listening to tapes, or watching Catholic DVDs or TV. How can we appreciate the real wonder of the Mass if we know nothing about it?

2. Read the Scripture readings before you go to Mass - Read them during the week, or on the morning before you go. Think about what they mean, and what significance they have for your life. This simple habit makes it much easier to appreciate the readings during Mass, and to get more out of the sermon.

3. Arrive early - We can't settle and pray during Mass if we rush in at the last minute or arrive late. Leave home extra early, and actually plan to have ten minutes in the Church before Mass starts. Kneel and worship the Lord; sit quietly. Talk to him. Bring your needs and concerns to him. And ask him to help you pray wholeheartedly during the Mass. You will notice the difference in your attention and in the spiritual fruits you receive if you do this regularly.

4. Really listen and pray during the Mass - It's so easy to drift through the Mass, to daydream, to let ourselves be distracted, to spend time mentally criticising the liturgy or the music or the priest... If we make a determined decision to concentrate and listen and be mentally and spiritually present, it really helps. We can imagine that the words are spoken for us - which they are. We can give our full attention to the scripture readings. And when Christ is made Really Present at the Consecration, when the bread and wine are changed into his Body and Blood, then we can welcome and adore him. And in this way, everything that happens becomes personal and precious.

5. Pray in thanksgiving after Mass - Don't rush out as soon as Mass has finished. Pray in your place for a few minutes. Thank God for all you have received during the Mass. Worship him with the angels and saints, who are mysteriously present in the church. And ask his help to live your faith as you go back into ordinary life.

FIVE INSPIRING CHRISTIAN TRUTHS

This is not a Creed, or even a list of all the important Christian doctrines. You need to get a Catechism for that. This is just a list of some Christian truths that are absolutely basic, and which help us in our ordinary lives if we can remember them often.

1. God is our Loving Father - There is a God. He is infinite love, infinite goodness; he is infinitely powerful. He created the world through love, and he watches over and guides everything that happens (this is the doctrine of 'Providence'). Nothing happens without some reason. Even every sin or failure, if we repent and bring it to Christ, can be given meaning and lead to good. It makes such a difference to know that every person, every moment, every event, is in God's loving hands.

2. Jesus is our Saviour - We can't save ourselves from sin and death; we find it hard even to be kind to each other. Jesus Christ is the one Saviour. He is true God and true man. He came into the world to forgive us our sins, to reveal the heart of God, and to lead us through death to eternal life with the Father. He gives us the gift of the Holy Spirit so that we can share in the divine life of the Most Holy Trinity even now on this earth. Jesus loves you and cares for you. You never need to feel alone. He is present with you always. Nothing can separate you from the love of Christ. Even sin, if we repent and ask for his help, is not a barrier. If we really knew and believed in the love of Christ, it would transform our lives.

3. The Power of the Holy Spirit is Given to Us - The love of the Holy Spirit, who is true God, has been poured into our hearts. We were given him at our Baptism and Confirmation; and this gift is renewed through all the sacraments, and through our faith. He makes us holy, and transforms us from the inside, so that we can share with him in the eternal love between the Father and the Son. We can call on him at any time, especially when we are weak, or when we need guidance and wisdom. He helps us to love, to pray, to cope with our difficulties. The Holy Spirit gives us incredible power, if only we would turn to him and trust in him. Whatever situation you are in, pray to the Holy Spirit to give you the spiritual gifts you need to do good and to do God's will. He will always help.

4. The Catholic Church is our True Spiritual Home - There are many different 'versions' of Christianity today, and sometimes we wonder where we should belong. The various Christian churches and communities have many good and holy things, that can lead to salvation, but only in the Catholic Church can we discover all the blessings and gifts that Christ wishes to give us. The Church that Christ founded is still found today in the Catholic Church. Through the Catholic Church we receive the life of Christ in the sacraments; we hear the teaching of Christ through the bishops and the Pope; and we share in the great Tradition of Christian faith that stretches back through the centuries. Trust the Church - even if there are some things that confuse you. Love the Church - even if there are things you struggle with. Be proud of your Catholic faith. Keep your Catholic identity. Be faithful to the teaching of the Catholic Church in your own life, and if necessary defend it in front of others. The Church is a rock, a foundation; a spiritual home that will always be a place of safety and security. We should never abandon it.

5. The Blessed Virgin Mary is our Mother - Mary is the one who gave Christ to the world; who supported him throughout his life; who shared in his Sacrifice on Calvary; and who was given by Jesus to the Beloved Disciple to be his spiritual mother. In the same way, now in heaven, Mary is a true mother to everyone who loves her son. She loves you and cares for you; she prays for you. You are her dear child. Turn to her often - for help and prayer, or simply for company and consolation. Her maternal love is one of the greatest gifts God has given us. Her prayers are more powerful than any of the other saints.

HOW TO GIVE YOUR LIFE TO GOD

Even though your faith may be weak, and you may have lots of doubts, the most important decision you can make is to give your life to God. If you were baptised as a child, then your parents have already done this for you. But as we get older we need to take this step for ourselves. It makes such a difference.

How do we do this, practically? When you are at church, or in the privacy of your own room, kneel down and tell God, in your own words, that you give your life to him. Tell him that you believe in his Son, Jesus Christ - even if your faith is still unclear. Tell him you want to do his will. There are so many other things to say, but they can follow at a later time.

The first step is simply to give our lives to God. When we do this, our lives will change. We may not feel any different, but gradually we will notice the presence of God in our lives more and more. We will see his power and his love at work in our lives. Unexpectedly, he will send us help, just at the right time, in the form of events or people or new opportunities or new desires. And our faith, gradually, will grow stronger.

If you are not sure what to say, perhaps these words of Blessed Charles de Foucauld will help:

Father, I abandon myself into your hands;
do with me what you will.
Whatever you may do, I thank you.
I am ready for all, I accept all.
Let only your will be done in me,
and in all your creatures;
I wish no more than this, O Lord.

Into your hands I commend my soul;
I offer it to you with all the love of my heart,
for I love you Lord,
and so need to give myself,
to surrender myself into your hands,
without reserve,
and with boundless confidence;
for you are my Father.

God created you for a purpose. He loves you and cares
for you. And he is closer to you than you can imagine.
You will never find true peace or true happiness
without him. As St Augustine wrote: "Lord, you have
made us for yourself; and our hearts are restless until
they rest in you".

- How to Pray -

FIVE WAYS OF PRAYING

At some stage in your spiritual life, you will want to make a bit more time for prayer each day. If you leave it to chance, it probably won't happen. The best way is to set aside a short time for prayer, at a particular time in the day, and stick to that time. Sometimes we feel like it, sometimes we don't. What matters is simply to be there, with the Lord. If one time doesn't work, then try another; and gradually God will help you to find a routine that suits you. But what do we do in that time? Here are five suggestions:

1. 'Formal' Prayers - There are many prayers in the Bible and in the Christian tradition that we can use in our own personal prayer. For example: the Our Father, the Hail Mary, the Glory Be, the Creeds, the morning offering, an act of contrition, the Psalms, the well-known prayers composed by the saints. It is good to have a book that contains different prayers we can use. These prayers help us to enter into the depths of Christian prayer. They take us beyond our own personal concerns, or help us to express concerns we didn't know we had. The important thing is to pray them with sincerity, with attention, with our whole heart and mind - and not just to rush through them.

2. Talking to God - Talk to him, in your own words, as you would to a close friend or a loving parent. Be completely honest, and natural. Tell him what you are thinking and feeling. Tell him your hopes and your fears and your worries. Ask him to help you and those you care for. Entrust your intentions to him. Pray for the needs of the Church and of the world. He always listens to us. And he always answers us in some way - even if that answer may be difficult to hear or to understand.

3. Sacred Scripture - God speaks to us through the Bible, and his Son Jesus is present with us as we read and meditate on his Holy Word. There are many ways of using the Bible in personal prayer: We can read through one of the books of the Bible; we can turn to our favourite passages; we can choose a certain story or a parable or a psalm. Here is one method, which is a form of '*lectio divina*' (holy reading): Choose a short passage (perhaps from one of the Gospels; perhaps the reading from Mass for that day); read it slowly; then have some time to think and pray about it. What strikes you? What interests you? What seems relevant to your life? Then read the passage again slowly. Have another time to think and reflect. And finally, talk to God about what you are thinking and feeling, and ask his help in your life. If this method is useful, you could work through one of the gospels taking another passage each day. It is also useful to use a

Catholic commentary or Bible guide (like 'Bible Alive') to help us understand the passages.

4. The Rosary - Praying the rosary keeps us close to God and to Our Lady, and keeps us rooted in the central truths of our Christian faith. When we say the individual prayers, we lift our hearts and minds to God. As we meditate on the mysteries of the rosary, we remember the life of Christ and of his Blessed Mother. Mary herself, in many apparitions, has asked us to pray the rosary, and promised that we will receive great graces if we do. Praying the rosary has kept the faith of many individuals and families alive, and helped their lives to be transformed. It is traditional to try and pray five decades each day. But some people find this too hard. Why not try and pray one decade each day (1 Our Father, 10 Hail Marys, 1 Glory Be), and make this a part of your daily prayer. It will make such a difference to your life and faith.

5. Silence - We can end up 'doing' and 'saying' a lot in our prayer time, but we also need some time of silence, so we can listen to our own hearts, so we can listen to God, and so we can simply be in his presence and appreciate who he is. Silence is hard, because we fidget, and our minds and hearts get easily distracted. But it doesn't matter if we get a bit distracted. What matters is that we make a bit of space for the Lord, and try and be still before him, and rest our hearts in him. We might feel peaceful or agitated or bored, but at least we have given him this space, and tried to let go of our busyness and noise. If we make a little time for silent prayer each day, then the Lord will help us to become more sensitive to his presence, and our prayer will become deeper and more intimate.

If you are not sure how to use your time of prayer, why not try the following: Set aside perhaps 15 minutes to pray in the morning. Close the door of your room. Keep some 'sacred space' in your room where you have a crucifix, some holy pictures, some holy water, and perhaps a candle. Kneel here. Begin by making the Sign of the Cross, and then pray some formal prayers, such as the Morning Offering, the Our Father, the Hail Mary, and the Glory Be. Then have a few moments talking to God in your own words, telling him all that is on your mind and heart, and asking for his help. Then have five minutes reflecting on a passage of the Bible - sit down if it helps you to be comfortable. Then have a few moments of silence. And finish by praying one decade of the Rosary. Don't rush or force anything. If you drop one thing, and spend more time on another, that is fine. The important thing is just to pray, and a structure is only something to help us get going.

FIVE ELEMENTS OF PRAYER

These are not 'methods'; they are different ways of 'relating' to God in prayer. We need to make sure that somehow, in our prayer each day and each week, we are relating to God in all these different ways.

1. Adoration - We worship and adore God for who he is, and not just for what he gives us. We praise him for his goodness and beauty and love. We adore him through Jesus Christ, and with the whole Church. Singing helps us to praise God. The Psalms are full of praise.

2. Repentance - Every day, we need to admit our sins and weaknesses, and ask for God's mercy and help. And we can ask for God's forgiveness for all sinners, especially those most in need of his mercy. These prayers of sorrow and contrition bring us joy and peace, because by turning to God in weakness, we allow his power and love to work in our lives.

3. Thanksgiving - We thank God for who he is, and for what he has done for us. We need to thank him in very particular ways for the blessings he has given us, even if things do not seem to be going well. To 'count our blessings' is an act of thanksgiving. Grateful people are full of joy.

4. Intercession - Jesus tells us, in the Gospels: "Ask!" We need to ask God the Father to help us in all our needs: big things; small things; everyday things; spiritual things. We are his children, and we should come to him with childlike simplicity, asking him to give us what we need and what we desire - as long as it is according to his will. We should put these requests into words, not because he is unaware of them, but because he wants us to express our needs and show him how much we trust him. The answer may come much later than we want, or in an unexpected way - but it will always come.

5. Contemplation - The first four types of prayer all involve us doing something: adoring, saying sorry, giving thanks, interceding. In contemplation, we are still before the Lord. But in that stillness, because of our faith, and our union with Jesus, we share in the life of God himself, of the Most Holy Trinity. We gaze at him, with the eyes of faith; we wonder about him; we become aware, very quietly, of his presence in the world, in the sacraments, and within our souls. Whenever we let go of our own activity, and step into the mystery of God, then we are allowing him to lead us on the great journey of contemplation.

Five fundamental Catholic prayers

It helps us to memorise certain prayers, so that we can use them at different times of the day and of the week, and so that our own personal prayer does not become too narrow. These prayers are especially useful and powerful when we do not know how to pray; or when we are worried or afraid; or when we are facing special trials or temptations. There are many prayers worth memorising - the more the better! Here are five essential prayers to memorise and use.

1. The Sign of the Cross - In the name of the Father, and of the Son, and of the Holy Spirit. Amen. [Cross yourself by using your right hand to touch your forehead, then your chest, then your left shoulder, and then your right shoulder].

2. The Our Father - Our Father, who art in heaven, hallowed be thy name. Thy kingdom come, thy will be done, on earth as it is in heaven. Give us this day our daily bread and forgive us our trespasses, as we forgive those who trespass against us. And lead us not into temptation, but deliver us from evil. Amen.

3. The Hail Mary - Hail Mary, full of grace, the Lord is with thee. Blessed art thou among women, and blessed is the fruit of thy womb, Jesus. Holy Mary, mother of God, pray for us sinners now and at the hour of our death. Amen.

4. The Glory Be - Glory be to the Father, and to the Son, and to the Holy Spirit. As it was in the beginning, is now, and ever shall be, world without end. Amen.

5. The Apostles' Creed - I believe in God the Father almighty, creator of heaven and earth. I believe in Jesus Christ, his only Son, our Lord. He was conceived by the power of the Holy Spirit and born of the Virgin Mary. He suffered under Pontius Pilate, was crucified, died, and was buried. He descended to the dead. On the third day he rose again. He ascended into heaven and is seated at the right hand of the Father. He will come again to judge the living and the dead. I believe in the Holy Spirit, the holy catholic Church, the communion of saints, the forgiveness of sins, the resurrection of the body, and the life everlasting. Amen. (There are slightly different translations of the Apostles' Creed. This is the modern one used in the *Catechism*).

FIVE OTHER IMPORTANT PRAYERS

Here are five other extremely useful prayers, which you can gradually memorise.

1. Come Holy Spirit - Come, O Holy Spirit, fill the hearts of your faithful, and enkindle in them the fire of your love. [Verse] Send forth your Spirit, and they shall be created. [Response] And you shall renew the face of the earth. Let us pray: O God, who has taught the hearts of the faithful by the light of the Holy Spirit, grant that by the gift of the same Spirit we may be always truly wise and ever rejoice in his consolation. Through Christ our Lord. Amen.

2. Hail, Holy Queen - Hail, Holy Queen, Mother of Mercy; hail our life, our sweetness, and our hope! To thee do we cry, poor banished children of Eve. To thee do we send up our sighs, mourning and weeping in this vale of tears. Turn then, most gracious advocate, thine eyes of mercy towards us, and after this, our exile, show unto us the blessed fruit of thy womb, Jesus. O clement, O loving, O sweet Virgin Mary. [Verse] Pray for us, O holy Mother of God. [Response] That we may be made worthy of the promises of Christ.

3. The Memorare - Remember, O most loving Virgin Mary, that it is a thing unheard of, that anyone ever had recourse to your protection, implored your help, or sought your intercession, was left forsaken. Filled therefore with confidence in your goodness I fly to you, O Mother, Virgin of virgins. To you I come, before you I stand, a sorrowful sinner. Despise not my poor words, O Mother of the Word Incarnate, but graciously hear and answer my prayer. Amen.

4. Prayer for the dead - Eternal rest grant unto them, O Lord, and let perpetual light shine upon them. May they rest in peace. Amen. (And make the sign of the cross at the same time).

5. Prayer to your Guardian Angel - Angel of God, my guardian dear, to whom God's love commits me here; ever this day be at my side, to light and guard, to rule and guide. Amen.

FIVE PRAYERS FOR PARTICULAR TIMES IN THE DAY

Here are five other prayers to say during the day.

1. A morning offering - O Jesus, through the Immaculate Heart of Mary, I offer you my prayers, works, joys, and sufferings of this day, in union with the holy sacrifice of the Mass throughout the world. I offer them for all the intentions of your Sacred Heart, and for the intentions of the Holy Father. Help me not to sin today. Help me to love you, and to love my neighbour, and to do your holy will in all things. Amen. (There are many versions of this prayer, but the main idea is simply to start each day by offering everything that will happen during the day to God).

2. The Angelus - The Angel of the Lord declared to Mary: And she conceived of the Holy Spirit. *Hail Mary, etc…* Behold the handmaid of the Lord: Be it done to me according to your word. *Hail Mary*, etc … And the Word was made Flesh: And dwelt among us: *Hail Mary*, etc … Pray for us, O holy Mother of God: That we may be made worthy of the promises of Christ. Let us pray: Pour forth, we beseech you, O Lord, your grace into our hearts, that we, to whom the Incarnation of Christ, your Son, was made known by the message of an angel, may be brought by his passion and cross to the glory of his resurrection, through the same Christ our Lord. Amen. May the divine assistance remain always with us, and may the souls of the faithful departed, through the mercy of God, rest in peace. Amen. (To remind us that God the Son became man for our salvation. Traditionally said in the morning, at midday, and in the early evening. It is customary to genuflect at the phrase 'And the Word was made Flesh').

3. Grace before meals - Bless us, O Lord, and these thy gifts, which we are about to receive from thy bounty, through Christ our Lord. Amen.

4. Thanksgiving after meals - We give you thanks, almighty God, for these and all your benefits, who live and reign, world without end. Amen. (It is customary then to pray for the dead). May the souls of the faithful departed, through the mercy of God, rest in peace. Amen.

5. Commendation - (Just before going to sleep) Jesus, Mary and Joseph, I give you my heart and my soul. Jesus, Mary and Joseph, assist me in my final agony. Jesus, Mary and Joseph, may I breathe forth my soul in peace with you.

FIVE 'ACTS' TO MAKE FREQUENTLY

In the tradition of Catholic prayers an 'act' is a prayer in which we express our conviction about something. When we make an 'act' we strengthen this conviction and it becomes more a part of us. It's like telling someone that we love them: This is not just passing on information, it actually makes the love more real and powerful. We can make these 'acts' at any time. We should especially make them when our conviction is weak or even disappearing, because that is just when we need to renew them. For example, if you feel your faith is weak or even non-existent, that is the very time to make an act of faith - even though we don't feel like it. This is not hypocrisy. Praying an 'act' allows us to touch something deeper than our feelings, and strengthens and renews that hidden conviction.

1. An act of faith - My God, I believe in you and all that your Church teaches, because you have said it, and your word is true.

2. An act of hope - My God, I hope in you, for grace and for glory, because of your promises, your mercy, and your power.

3. An act of charity - My God, because you are so good, I love you with all my heart, and for your sake, I love my neighbour as myself.

4. An act of contrition - O my God, because you are so good, I am very sorry that I have sinned against you; and I promise that with the help of your grace, I will not sin again. Amen.

5. An act of entrustment to the Sacred Heart - Sacred Heart of Jesus, I put my trust in thee. Sacred Heart of Jesus, have mercy on me.

- How to be Holy -

FIVE SPIRITUAL PRACTICES

You can gradually make these practices a part of your everyday life.

1. Arrow prayers - Whenever you remember, in the course of your ordinary activities, say a short prayer in your own heart to the Lord. The simpler the better: 'Lord, help me!' or 'Jesus, I love you' or 'Have mercy on us, Lord'. It is like sending an arrow up to heaven. It helps us to remember God and to connect with him even when we are busy with ordinary things. And these prayers have an effect: He hears us and gives us his extra help.

2. 'Offering up' - Whenever you meet some difficulty or suffering or disappointment, big or small, then 'offer it up' to God. Simply say in your heart, 'Lord, I offer you this', or 'I accept this suffering and offer it to you'. In this way, even if we don't use all these words, we are uniting our lives and our sufferings with the sacrifice of Jesus on the cross, and they become part of his prayer for the salvation of the world. This means that our difficulties and sufferings, which seem to be such a pain and a burden, take on a whole new meaning: they become a powerful prayer to help countless unknown people.

Nothing is wasted. And our own acceptance helps us
to grow in humility and holiness, and keeps us from
the dangers of anger or despair. We can also offer up
our sufferings for special intentions; and it helps if we
name these intentions as we are praying - e.g., to help
us conquer a particular sin, or to help in the conversion
of a needy person. This practice does not mean that we
become passive and stop trying to change things - often,
when we meet suffering or difficulty (in our own lives
or in the lives of others) it is our responsibility to try
and change things and put things right. But in the very
moment when we meet that suffering or difficulty, that is
when we can offer it up. And if, for whatever reason, we
have to live with it for longer, then we keep offering it up.

3. Fasting - This is one of the great spiritual and
Christian traditions. Whenever we fast we unite ourselves
with the sufferings of Jesus and of the whole world;
we learn to let go of our attachments to sin and self-
indulgence; and we learn a deeper gratitude for the gifts
God has given us. In practice, what is fasting? It takes
different forms. The simplest form, recommended by
the Church, is to miss one proper meal and substitute it
with something small, e.g. with bread and water. This
can be done on Fridays. We should not fast in a way that
damages our health or makes us less able to work and
care for those around us. We should talk to someone wise

about fasting before we begin, to make sure that we are fasting in a way that is suitable for us. (We can also fast from other activities: TV, Internet, telephone...) We are obliged as Catholics to abstain from meat on Fridays, or to do some other act of penance or some special good work, in honour of Our Lord's Passion.

4. 'The Little Way' - This is the spirituality developed by St Thérèse of Lisieux, where we do the small things of everyday life with great love. In her view, the secret of holiness is not to achieve great and dramatic things (which can make us proud); it is to do small and hidden things with care and kindness and humility, for the love of God and for the love of our neighbour. Whatever is happening in our life, whatever our work or studies or family situation, wherever we find ourselves, there are always opportunities to act with love and kindness. Instead of wishing we were somewhere else, or even wishing we were someone else - the secret of holiness is to love in our present situation. God is here! This doesn't stop us making changes or moving on when the time is right; but it does mean we are more open to his will in the present moment.

5. Recollection - This is a word used a lot in the spiritual tradition. It means that we are aware of ourselves and aware of God's presence in our lives; we are mentally

and spiritually 'awake'; we have a kind of inner peace
and stillness and attentiveness; we are not completely
distracted and caught up in our own activity or thoughts
or daydreams. You know when we are very busy and
we suddenly 'snap out of it' and become aware of
ourselves and our surroundings: this is the beginning
of recollection, but it goes much deeper than that. We
should value the gift of recollection, and try to be as
recollected as possible - because then we are more
sensitive to everything around us, to God, and to our
conscience. Sometimes we can't help getting busy
because of some work or conversation. This doesn't
matter - we just try and restore our recollection as soon as
possible. But at other times the inner busyness is our own
fault: because we are rushing or being careless; because
there is too much noise in our lives (music, computers,
videos); or because we never stop to pray.

FIVE CHRISTIAN RESPONSIBILITIES

We have many different responsibilities as Christians.
Here are just five to make you think.

1. Learn about your faith - If we want to have a strong
faith then we need to learn more about it. We spend
hours learning about other things that interest us - why
not learn about our Catholic faith? Get some good books.
Find some good websites. Go to a good discussion group

or prayer group that has some input. Do a course in the Catholic faith or in catechesis.

2. Evangelise - This means literally 'sharing the Gospel'. We don't all have to go out into the streets and tell people about Jesus. But we do all have a responsibility to witness to our faith in everyday life, and to share our faith with others when the opportunity occurs. Simple tips: Don't hide your faith. If a conversation arises when religion or faith is the topic, don't be shy about sharing your own beliefs. And have the courage to start conversations; to ask people what they think and believe, so you can understand them, and have a chance to share your own faith. Better still, invite your friends to some Catholic events that are taking place - to a prayer group or retreat or young people's event. And pray. If you pray each morning for an opportunity to share your faith, you will be amazed how God will provide one - and it will seem like a miracle. We just need to be open, and brave. People are depending on us.

3. Get involved in the world - Get involved in the issues of the day, and in the issues of the world in which you live. Vote: In local and national elections. Get involved in the social and political issues of your school, your college, your workplace, your neighbourhood, your town, your country. Don't sit on the fence, or leave it to someone else. Don't hide away in a Christian bubble. We are meant to be light and leaven in the world. We don't just get involved 'as Christians' - we go in as ordinary people who have a stake in society, trying to be just and kind and fair. And sometimes our Christian values will be important, and we will need to stand up for them, and help others to see how needed they are. There is a great tradition in this country of lay Catholics being involved in politics - it is a wonderful vocation. But even if we are not 'politicians' we are still called to be political in the best sense of the word.

4. Support your parish - We support our parish simply by belonging and going to Sunday Mass and trying to be faithful Catholics. If we are over 18 we support the parish by making a financial offering at Mass each Sunday. If we pay tax, then it seems sensible to gift-aid it. There is a biblical tradition of 'tithing', of offering one tenth of our wages to the Church, and some Christians still follow this tradition. The important thing is to be generous in our giving, to set aside a generous offering each week, and not just to leave it to chance or to whatever is in our back pocket. Think about whether you could give perhaps not 10% ('tithing') but even 2% of your wages. And apart from money, we can support our parish in so many other ways: By volunteering when help is needed; by taking on a ministry if we are asked; by making constructive suggestions about what can be done in the parish; by loving and supporting our priests. We do not need to be 'busy' in the parish all the time, because we have many other responsibilities, but we do need to be generous with our time and energy.

5. Have a special concern for the poor - Look out for those in any kind of difficulty or need. Support them, in whatever way seems realistic, with your love and time and money and prayer. Those who are unnoticed or unpopular or unattractive; those who are lonely; the sick, the elderly; those with learning difficulties; the stranger, the newcomer, the one who cannot speak the right language. Those without homes or families or jobs. Those without faith or love or hope. We should have a special concern for the poor. We find Christ in them, and we bring the love of Christ to them - so that Christ is 'all in all'. Generosity and self-sacrifice are two of the greatest Christian virtues - and deep down we are far happier when we are giving than when we are taking. But the real issue is love: To love all those we meet, with a sincere and kind and tender heart.

FIVE WAYS TO SANCTIFY YOUR HOME OR ROOM

The most important way to sanctify your home is to sanctify yourself! To live a holy life. But these Catholic customs can also help us to make our home or personal room a place of holiness and peace.

1. Have your home or room blessed - Ask your local priest to come and bless your home or room. He will be happy to do so. This blessing 'consecrates' your home so that it is a place dedicated to God; it drives away evil spirits.

2. Hang a crucifix on your wall - Of the many symbols of Christian faith, this is the most important one. By placing a crucifix on the wall it reminds us and other people of our Saviour's love for us. And it reminds us to turn to him in prayer.

3. Keep some holy water - You can get some holy water from the church and keep it in a bottle or some kind of holder or holy water 'stoop'. When you pray, bless yourself with this holy water by dipping your finger in it and making the sign of the cross. This is not a superstition, it is a 'sacramental': it allows God's power to work in our lives, through the blessing that the priest has given to the water, and through our faith.

4. Keep a 'sacred space' in your room - This does not need to be a large space! It just means that we have a small area in our room, a focus, where we have (perhaps) some holy pictures, an open Bible, a candle, etc. This place can then be a focus for our prayer, and a reminder of what is important in our lives.

5. Consecrate your home to the Sacred Heart of Jesus
- There are special prayers you can make to consecrate
your home to the Sacred Heart - look on the internet, or
ask for information in a Catholic bookshop. The important
thing is simply to dedicate your home to the Sacred
Heart, and to hang an image of the Sacred Heart on your
wall. You can get special images which have a prayer of
consecration written on them.

FIVE THINGS TO BE

This is going to sound like a bad song…

1. Be happy - True joy is not just a mood that comes and
goes, it is a gift that comes with faith, because we know
that we are loved by God, that we are his children, and
that he is guiding our lives. Joy is a gift that the Holy
Spirit has already given us; and sometimes we need to be
more open to it, and actively let go of the things that stop
us being joyful: negativity, fear, resentment, self-doubt,
and even despair. And joy is a gift that we can choose
to give to others, overcoming our own feelings and
trying to be joyful for their sake. This is not being false,
it is giving a gift to others even if we don't yet possess
it ourselves. So be happy! And bring that happiness to
others as a gift.

2. Be normal - Don't become a weird, intense Catholic who only ever talks about Catholic issues and only ever does Catholic activities. We are meant to enjoy life and live it to the full; to appreciate and value all the truly good things of the world; to be friends with those who have faith and those who have none; to build God's Kingdom wherever we are. The only thing we need to avoid is sin and the 'occasions' of sin.

3. Be yourself - Always be yourself, in front of God and others. Never do things to impress people, especially not spiritual things. Trust that God created you and loves you as you are (apart from your sins), and be brave enough to be yourself. Of course we have to be polite or give way or make allowances for others sometimes, but this is different from being false.

4. Be honest - Be completely honest with yourself. Be completely honest with God. There is no need to pretend. Be honest about your hopes and dreams and fears and worries. Be honest about your sins and stupidities, and about your gifts and passions. Only then can we learn to grow and move forward. Only then can God touch and heal what is broken, and develop what is good, and give what is needed.

5. Be a saint - There is no other way of finding true joy and happiness. There is no other way of doing lasting good for others. There is nothing more important than a life of sanctity, because only the saints know what is truly important.

FIVE SAINTS FOR YOUNG PEOPLE

The saints give us their friendship, their example, and their prayers. They are alive now in heaven; and we are connected to them because we all belong together to the Body of Christ. This is not a superstition - it is a reality. We can talk to them at any time; and ask for their help and friendship. How do we pray to the saints? The simplest way is just to say: "Saint (*Name*): Pray for us". There are many saints who died young, or who had a special love for young people. Here are five who have a special concern for young people.

1. St Joseph - Because every list of saints should include St Joseph, husband of the Virgin Mary, foster-father of Jesus, patron of the Universal Church.

2. St John Bosco [1815-1888] - Spent his whole life as a priest working with young people and leading them to Christ.

3. St Thérèse of Lisieux [1873-1897] - Carmelite nun who led a profound life of love and prayer in her enclosed convent. She developed her 'Little Way' of holiness, which involved doing small and hidden things with great love.

4. St Maria Goretti [1890-1902] - Died at the age of twelve after she was attacked by a young man trying to rape her. In hospital, just before her death, she forgave him, and asked God to forgive him.

5. Blessed Pier Giorgio Frassati [1901-1925] - Engineering student with many friends and a great love of life. Was involved in politics, hidden charitable work, and Christian movements. Died at the age of twenty-four from a disease he caught while visiting the poor.

FIVE GREAT SAINTS OF THE TWENTIETH CENTURY

There are so many recent saints to choose from - it's good to see authentic photographs of them, to realise they were real people. Here are five of the best known and loved that you can pray to.

1. St Maximilian Kolbe - Franciscan priest and martyr, who did so much work to spread the faith through the communications media (publishing, magazines, radio etc); and to spread devotion to Mary Immaculate. Killed in Auschwitz after he offered his life to be taken in place of another man's.

2. St Teresa Benedicta of the Cross (Edith Stein) - Jewish philosopher; convert to Catholicism; and Carmelite nun. She was in Holland when the Dutch bishops, together with other Christians, protested against the Nazi treatment of the Jews. As a result of these protests, Catholics of Jewish descent were arrested, and Edith was killed in Auschwitz.

3. St Pio of Pietrelcina (Padre Pio) - Franciscan priest with many spiritual gifts (stigmata, reading souls, bilocation, prophesy). Renowned for his work in the confessional, and his spiritual wisdom.

4. St Gianna Molla: Wife, mother and doctor - When pregnant with her fourth child, she was found to have a growth on her uterus, and she had to choose whether to have an operation that would mean the loss of her baby, in order to increase the chances of her own survival, or whether to have a less effective operation and save her baby. She chose the less effective one, lived for the duration of the pregnancy, and died days after the birth.

Blessed Mother Teresa of Calcutta - Teaching nun who discovered her 'vocation within a vocation', to serve the poorest of the poor in Calcutta and throughout the world. Founder of the Missionaries of Charity who continue her work.

- How to go to Confession -

HOW TO GO TO CONFESSION: THE BASICS

There are variations in the way different priests celebrate the sacrament of confession, and they will sometimes introduce different prayers and scripture readings. Here is the traditional way of making a confession, which has the very basics of what we need to know and say. If you want to know more about the kind of life we should be living as Christians, and what sins we should be avoiding, see the 'Examination of Conscience' below.

1. General advice - Sometimes we get nervous about going to confession. But don't let nerves or fear hold you back. However long it has been, however bad the sin, however embarrassed you feel - don't let anything stop you from going to confession.

Remember that it is the Lord we meet in confession. Priests are all different; and some we like more than others. But what matters is the presence of Jesus in our life through the ministry of the priest, and not the personality of the priest. Christ touches our life through each priest, whoever he is; and every priest will keep your confession absolutely secret for the rest of his life.

Your local parish should have confessions at least once a week. It is also useful to know the times of confession at other churches nearby, or at churches near where you work or study. The diocesan Cathedral is often a good place to go to confession, with plenty of different times.

You have the right as a Catholic to go to confession 'anonymously', in a confessional where the priest cannot identify you. If your local parish does not have this, then if you prefer you can try and find confession at another parish that does. Try to go regularly, perhaps every month.

Briefly examine your conscience at the end of each day, and make an act of contrition. In this way you will become more sensitive to what is really happening in your own life, and you will be more prepared and more honest as you come to confession.

2. Before confession - Spend a few minutes before your confession: Pray for God's help and guidance; examine your conscience; remember any sins you have committed (write them down if it helps); pray for God's forgiveness.

But don't spend forever trying to remember every little sin (this can become an obsession that is called 'scruples') - ten minutes is probably a good amount of time; an hour is too long.

It is our duty to mention in confession all our serious (or 'mortal') sins; and we are encouraged to mention some of our other smaller (or 'venial') sins and everyday faults, but we don't need to list every minor failure. Remember that all our venial sins are forgiven and forgotten whenever we pray for God's forgiveness, and whenever we receive holy communion. If you are not sure what to say or do, don't worry - tell the priest, and ask him to help you as you begin.

3. In confession - Begin by saying: "In the name of the Father, and of the Son, and of the Holy Spirit. Amen." Then add: "Bless me, Father, for I have sinned. It is (state the length of time) since my last confession". Then tell him very briefly what you are doing in life, to help him understand your situation; e.g. "I am at school studying for A-levels" or "I am a wife and mother".

Now confess your sins. Be simple and straightforward. Just put into words what you have done wrong since you last went to confession. Don't make excuses; but if it helps, say a little bit about what happened and why. When you have finished, say: "I am sorry for all these sins and the sins of my past life".

The priest might then talk to you and give you some advice. He will give you a penance to do (a prayer or action that expresses your sorrow and your desire to live a new life).

The priest will then ask you to make an Act of Contrition. Say one you know, or use the following one: "O my God, because you are so good, I am very sorry that I have sinned against you; and I promise that with the help of your grace, I will not sin again. Amen."

The priest then says the prayer of absolution, which is the moment when God forgives your sins. He may add some other prayers as well.

4. After confession - If it is possible now, do your penance in the church before you leave; e.g. if you have been asked to say a certain prayer, kneel down and say it now.

Pray for a moment in thanksgiving for the forgiveness you have received in this sacrament; and pray for God's help to live a new life.

You might feel relieved and peaceful and full of joy. Or you might feel dry and empty. It doesn't really matter. What matters is that we have been forgiven and been given new life. The Lord has touched us - even if we do not feel it. That knowledge should give us a kind of inner peace and joy, even if we don't feel it.

If you forgot to mention something small, don't get all worried. In confession the Lord forgives all the sins that we intended to mention (as long as we did not deliberately conceal anything).

EXAMINATION OF CONSCIENCE

An Examination of Conscience is simply a list of some of the ways that we can love God and our neighbour, and some of the ways we can fail to love through sin. Reflecting on an Examination of Conscience helps us to be honest with ourselves and honest with God. It is not meant to be a burden. It helps us to examine our lives, and to make a good confession, so that we can be at peace with Christ and with one another. The important thing, of course, is to love, and to live our Catholic faith with our whole heart. But now and then it is useful to spell out what this really means, and to make sure that we are not kidding ourselves.

This Examination of Conscience is not to be used every day, or even at every confession - we do not need to go through a checklist every time. It is here for us to look at every now and then. It is based around the *Ten Commandments*. As we reflect on it, we can ask the Lord to shine his light into our hearts. Some things will not apply to us; but if something in particular touches our conscience, then we can bring it to confession.

Above all, let us remember God's mercy and his love for us. His love never fails or changes. He loves us passionately, with infinite kindness and tenderness. The only reason we remember our sins is so that we can turn to him and receive his forgiveness, and learn to love him in a new and deeper way.

I am the Lord your God. You shall not have strange gods before me (1st Comm); You shall not take the name of the Lord your God in vain (2nd Comm).
Do I seek to love God with all my heart?

Do I stay faithful to Jesus, even when I have difficulties or doubts?

Do I make at least some time for prayer every day?

Do I hold on to the practice of my Catholic faith, or have I turned away from it, or spoken against the teachings of the Church?

Have I been involved with the occult, e.g., with ouija boards, séances, tarot cards, fortune-telling, or the like? Have I put faith in horoscopes?

Have I received Holy Communion in a state of mortal sin?

Have I lied to the priest in confession or deliberately not confessed a mortal sin?

Have I used God's holy name irreverently?

When things are difficult, do I hope in God, or do I give in to self-pity and despair? Do I get angry and resentful with him?

Remember to keep holy the Lord's Day (3rd Comm).
Have I deliberately missed Mass on Sundays or Holy Days of Obligation?

Do I make a sincere effort to come to Mass on time, and to listen and pray during the Mass? Do I fast for an hour before receiving Holy Communion (apart from water and medicine)? Am I reverent in church?

Do I try to keep Sunday as a day of prayer, rest and relaxation, avoiding unnecessary work?

Honour your father and your mother (4th Comm).

Do I honour and respect my parents? Do I show kindness to my brothers and sisters?

Do I treat my children with love and respect? Do I carry out my family duties?

Do I support and care for the well-being of all family members, especially the elderly and the sick?

Do I honour and obey my lawful superiors, and follow the just laws of my country?

You shall not kill (5th Comm).

Do I love my neighbour as myself? Do I try to be kind and generous with everyone I meet? Do I help those in need?

Do I harbour hatred or anger against anyone?

Do I try to forgive those who have hurt me? Do I pray for my enemies?

Have I deliberately tried to hurt anyone - physically or emotionally?

Have I had an abortion or encouraged another to have an abortion?

Have I attempted suicide?

Have I abused alcohol or used illegal drugs?

Have I led anyone to sin through bad example or through direct encouragement?

Do I care for my own physical, emotional, and spiritual health?

You shall not commit adultery (6th Comm); You shall not desire your neighbour's wife (9th Comm).

Am I faithful to my husband or wife, in my actions, my words, and my thoughts?

As a Catholic, was I married outside the Church?

Has our marriage been open to new life, or have I used contraception, or been sterilised?

Have I engaged in sexual activity before marriage or outside of marriage?

Do I view pornography on the TV or internet, or through videos or magazines?

Have I masturbated?

Have I used impure language or told impure jokes?

Do I dress and behave modestly? Am I respectful and chaste in my relationships?

Do I try to turn away from impure thoughts and temptations?

You shall not steal (7th Comm).

Have I stolen or accepted stolen goods?

Have I cheated anyone of what I owe them?

Am I lazy? Do I waste time at work or at school or college?

Do I gamble excessively?

Do I share what I have with the poor and with the Church according to my means?

Have I copied or used pirated material: videos, music, software?

You shall not bear false witness against your neighbour (8th Comm).

Do I tell the truth, even if it is inconvenient? Or do I lie or mislead people?

Am I a trustworthy and sincere person? Do I keep my word and my promises, and keep confidential things confidential?

Have I cheated in exams or been dishonest in any way in my studies?

Have I gossiped or spread rumours or spoken badly about people in any way? Have I ridiculed or humiliated anyone?

You shall not desire your neighbour's goods (10th Comm).

Am I grateful for the things I have and for the blessings God has given me? Or am I always complaining?

Am I jealous of other people: jealous of their possessions, talents, beauty, success or relationships?

Am I greedy or selfish? Am I too caught up with material things?

FIVE WAYS OF DEALING WITH
RECURRING TEMPTATIONS

Obviously we should be determined to resist them and turn away from them and avoid the situations where we meet them. But sometimes a bit more thought is needed too, especially when there is an

ongoing struggle. Within every temptation there is
an attraction to something good (pleasure, beauty,
companionship, excitement, etc.) that gets distorted
and misdirected. There is often a longing in the human
heart. We might be lonely or angry or afraid or just
hungry for something beyond ourselves, and we turn
to some momentary comfort in drink or pornography
or whatever. Then we can get dependent, trapped,
and even addicted to certain habits. But they leave
us empty, and they can damage us spiritually as
well as physically and mentally. Very often there is
some unaddressed need, some emotional or spiritual
difficulty that we are not facing. If the situation is very
serious, there are four steps that will really help us to
face and hopefully overcome these difficulties; and a
fifth step that will be invaluable for many people:

**1. Never forget that the Lord loves you and cares for
you** - The good news is that the Lord never abandons
us. He comes into our lives, into all the mess, bringing
consolation, hope, and strength. We need to turn to him
more and more, admitting our weakness. He may not
solve everything straight away, but if we stay close to
him, and are realistic about what needs to change, then he
will gradually help us to move forward.

2. Deepen your prayer life - Pray daily for God's help in this struggle, and for the help of Our Lady and of all the saints; and pray particularly in those times of difficulty and temptation. A short, simple prayer in times of temptation can make all the difference: 'Lord, have mercy' or 'Jesus, help me' or 'Mother Mary, pray for me'.

3. Talk to someone who is wise and trustworthy - Perhaps a good priest you know, perhaps someone else. There is nothing worse than being trapped in a sin or addiction and feeling alone with it; and there is nothing more helpful than sharing this difficulty with someone else, speaking honestly about our struggles, and asking for their prayers. The greatest ally of sin is secrecy.

4. Go to confession frequently - Perhaps every month. Confess these sins and struggles with honesty and simplicity. We do not need to stay away from confession just because we keep repeating the same sins - God's love and mercy are as great every time that we come to confession.

5. Join a support group - For many of us it will help enormously to join a group such as Alcoholics Anonymous or Narcotics Anonymous, where we can admit our need for help and receive support and encouragement. There are many different such groups.

Five common struggles

There are many temptations that we struggle against. Here are some of the common struggles that people face today. In all these situations we need to take the advice in the section above about 'recurring temptations'.

1. Alcohol - There is nothing wrong with alcohol in itself, and in the right measure it can bring joy and happiness. But for many people it becomes a temptation or an addiction, and it can begin to destroy our relationships and our lives. And many other sins result from the loss of self-control that alcohol brings on. Excessive drinking and drunkenness has become an almost normal part of life for many young people, and it is hard to stand against it. Be honest about your use of alcohol. If you are drinking too much; if it is making your life difficult; if you are becoming dependent on it; if you are not sure how to stop - then admit this, and try to get some help. For most of us, we simply need to be moderate in our drinking, and to decide on some guidelines. For example: not to get drunk; not to drink alone; not to drink just because we are unhappy or lonely or being pressured to drink.

2. Drugs - Some people believe that it is OK to use illegal 'recreational' drugs in moderation. But for Catholics it is wrong to use illegal drugs simply because they are illegal - that is the Catholic understanding of how we should respect and obey the just laws of our country. So if we have just experimented with some drugs in the past, and not taken it very seriously, we should be aware that it is a sin to take illegal drugs, and confess that drug use, and move on. But far more than that, drug use can become a habit and then an addiction that can ruin our lives in so many ways - our mental and physical health; our finances; our friendships; and our spiritual life. If you're not using drugs, then simply make a decision that you will not start, for any reason. The risks are too great. If you are using drugs occasionally, then make a decision to stop; go to confession; and be honest about the situations and friendships that drag you into using drugs, and change those situations if necessary. If you are in some kind of addiction, then seek the help outlined in the section above: talking, praying, confession and finding support.

3. Gambling - Gambling has always been a temptation, but it is even worse now because of the internet. In theory, there is nothing wrong with minor, occasional gambling, if we are not dependent on it, and if it is not using money that should be used for other things. But in practice gambling can easily become an unjust waste of money, it can betray a lack of trust in God, and it can turn into a desperate and dangerous addiction. If you are struggling with this, then be honest about the damage it is doing; and be realistic about the help you will need to overcome it and the life changes you may need to make. The simplest and safest answer is never to gamble.

4. Pornography - Our whole culture is highly eroticised. Explicit images which verge on the pornographic are a normal part of television and advertising. And pornography itself is easily available on the internet, on DVDs, in magazines, on satellite TV channels, and in many other places. The use of pornography does immense damage to the hearts and minds of those who turn to it, as well as to those involved in the pornographic 'industry'. Don't pretend, as many people would like us to believe, that it is just a natural and harmless pastime. If you are using pornography, then pray, talk to someone, and try to turn things around. Half the battle lies in avoiding the obvious 'occasions of sin'. Get rid of the films and magazines. If the temptations come from a computer or TV in your bedroom, then move it out - put it in the living room, or some place where you are not alone.

5. Masturbation - This is a real struggle for many people, young and old. Society tells us that masturbation is OK, that it's a natural expression of our sexuality. But the Church wisely teaches that it is wrong, and this fits with the experience of many people. Our sexuality, in its broadest sense, is meant to lead us to open and loving relationships with others; but masturbation traps us in ourselves and in our own sexual fantasies. It may provide some pleasure and momentary release, but it leaves us lonely and unfulfilled. We need to guard our thoughts and imaginations more carefully, and be courageous about turning away to something else when these temptations come. Once again, we need honesty, prayer and confession.

In all these situations, it is not just our own determination that matters, it is the love of God, which touches us and heals us and gives us hope. It is only his love that can satisfy the deepest hungers of our hearts. It is his love that gives us the courage to admit our weaknesses and the confidence to try and move forward. He wants us to be free!

FIVE THINGS TO AVOID

We shouldn't think too much about negative things. But here is a quick list of five things that a Christian should keep away from.

1. The Devil - Don't play with the Devil. He has been defeated by the Blood of Christ, but he can still cause great harm in the world and in our spiritual lives. Avoid sin. Don't make excuses for your sins. If temptations come, run away from them; turn your mind to other things; get out of this bad situation that is causing them. Don't waste time considering the temptation and weighing it up - you will only get drawn in. Avoid the occult: Don't get drawn into ouija boards, séances, tarot cards, fortune-telling, or the like. Don't be superstitious. If you are in any kind of spiritual difficulty or danger or temptation, the best and simplest response is to use the name of Jesus. Simply pray, 'Jesus, help me' - and the power of his Holy Name will protect you from evil.

2. Worry - Of course we get worried and afraid sometimes - it happens quite naturally. But worry can become a habit, or an obsession, or a superstition. Deep down, we do not need to be worried or anxious as Christians. God loves us; Christ has saved us; and he has promised to be with us and to guide us at every moment in our lives. Worry is often a sign that we do not trust God, or that we are clinging to our own hopes and plans. When you are worried, pray a prayer like this: "Lord, I trust you, and I believe in your goodness and power. I

give you my worries. Give me your peace, and help me to
trust you more."

3. Bad 'friends' - We are not saints ourselves, and we
should not expect all our friends to be saints. If they have
difficulties or weaknesses, we should stay by them. But
some 'friends' are not really friends - if they are living
very bad lives, and if they are drawing us into things
that are not good. We should never abandon someone
just because we disagree with them. But we need to
be honest about the effect that certain 'friendships' are
having on us. If they are actually taking us away from
Christ and from the life he wants us to live, then we
should see less of them, since the 'friendship' is not
doing us or them any good.

4. 'Occasions of sin' - This old-fashioned phrase is still
useful: It means any situation where we get tempted to
sin, where we get drawn into bad things. For example:
we use the internet late at night and so end up viewing
pornographic sites. Or we have a couple of drinks and so
end up getting argumentative and violent. Or we go out
with this group of friends and always end up getting into
trouble. Very often we sin not because we have some
big desire to sin, but because we find ourselves in a bad
situation and then we can't resist. The answer? Avoid the
situation that keeps happening, and then you will (usually)

avoid the sin. If we know that this situation is dangerous
for us, and we keep returning to it, then we become
even more responsible for the sins we are committing.

5. Extremes - We should be extremely passionate about
Christ and extremely committed to our Catholic faith.
But sometimes, especially when we are new to our faith,
we can take things to extremes in an unhealthy way. For
example: We learn about fasting, but then fast so much
that it affects our health and our work and makes it hard
for us to be a loving, joyful Christian. Or we fall in love
with prayer, and think that the more we pray the better it
is - which is simply not true, because it is possible to pray
too much as well as too little. Or we become so interested
in our Catholic faith that we talk about it all the time to
friends and family (both Catholic and non-Catholic), so
that we bore them silly and even make the Catholic faith
seem unattractive because we have gone on so much. So
we must live things with great love and passion, but in
the right measure. If we are lukewarm and just beginning,
then we often do need to do more. But if we are already
living our faith and committed to it, then often we need to
go deeper rather than doing more.

- How to be Chaste -

MARRIAGE

This section is not by any means an explanation of the profound meaning of marriage. It simply tries to answer one or two questions that young people often have about the relationship between sex, marriage, chastity, and the Church's often misunderstood teaching about contraception. Nor does this section discuss the particular meaning of a Christian, sacramental marriage - where the natural love between husband and wife becomes an expression of the love of Christ for his Church: The Lord is present in every Christian marriage, helping husband and wife to love and to forgive; bringing them joy and strength and healing.

1. Sex and Marriage - Marriage is the complete and lifelong commitment between a man and a woman, when they promise to love each other wholeheartedly, to remain faithful to each for the rest of their lives, and to welcome children (if they are given that gift) and build a family together. Sex is the natural expression and fulfilment of all this; it unites a husband and wife in the closest intimacy, and it allows them to be open to the gift of a child.

2. The complete gift of one person to another - When a husband and wife make love, they are saying to each other: "I love you without reserve; I give you my whole self; I accept your gift of yourself to me; and together we are open to the gift of new life that may come from our love". So marriage is not just three human experiences that are accidentally combined (commitment and sex and children) - it is one reality, one gift, that has three essential and inseparable meanings. In other words, the love that is expressed in sexual union is meant to be lifelong and life-giving. This does not mean that all married couples will be able to have children, or that every time a couple make love they will conceive a child. It just means that in every act of sexual intercourse they are open and willing to conceive a child.

3. Chastity within Marriage - The profound meaning of sexual love within a marriage cannot be defined in terms of a set of moral rules - it is something far richer and more mysterious. But the wisdom of the Church and of Christian experience shows us that it is necessary to keep within some moral boundaries if a husband and wife are to be true to the meaning of their marriage. Adultery, obviously, is wrong - because it means we are not giving ourselves wholeheartedly to our husband or wife. But there are other ways that married couples can be unchaste or unfaithful to each other in their hearts.

4. Contraception - Using contraception, perhaps less obviously, is also wrong - because it means we are holding something back from a love that is meant to be total. Sexual love within marriage is meant to be a gift 'without reservation'. If a couple uses contraception it means that they are unwilling to share their fertility, their ability to give life. A life-giving relationship is artificially made sterile, and married love becomes less generous and even selfish. Contraception is an act 'against conception' - two people try to give themselves to each other completely in sexual intercourse, but in the same moment they take back something fundamental.

5. Natural Family Planning - Contraception is quite different from 'Natural Family Planning' (which is sometimes called 'Natural Fertility Awareness'), where for serious reasons a couple might try to avoid pregnancy at a certain time by abstaining from sex during the woman's fertile periods. In this case, the husband and wife are not holding anything back - they are just waiting for the right time to express that love in sexual intercourse. Natural Family Planning is morally acceptable because it does not act 'against' conception - it respects the freedom of the couple to abstain at certain times, and it respects the deepest meaning of married love and sexual intercourse.

THE MEANING OF CHASTITY

This section is not a full explanation of the meaning of chastity. It simply tries to put chastity in a positive light, and to answer a question that many young people find difficult to understand: Why does the Catholic Church teach that sex is only for within marriage? This only makes sense because of the understanding of marriage presented above.

1. Chastity and love - The human heart is made for love. Love touches every aspect of our lives - it touches our desires, our thoughts, our emotions, our plans. But love is not just a feeling that comes and goes. It is a relationship, a shared commitment, a responsibility. Chastity is about learning to love in a way that will bring us true happiness; it is about living our sexuality in a way that respects the deepest meaning of love. There are many ways of loving. There are also many ways that love can go wrong and become short-sighted or even destructive.

2. Chastity and freedom - Chastity is much more than a set of rules about what we can and can't do - it is having an inner freedom to love others without possessing them, to delight in others without using them, to care for others without smothering them. It requires a spirit of kindness, generosity, joy, humility, modesty, patience, self-sacrifice, common-sense, wisdom, prayer, and a sense of humour. Chastity keeps our love pure and unpossessive, and it keeps at bay the lust and selfishness that can damage our hearts and our relationships.

3. Struggling with chastity - Some habits harden our hearts and make it harder for us to love others in a chaste way (pornography, sexual fantasizing, masturbation). Some ways of behaving distort our relationships (dressing immodestly, looking lustfully at others, flirting). Whatever our particular struggles with chastity, three things will always help us: Talking things through honestly with someone wise and trustworthy (there is nothing worse than trying to deal with these issues alone); praying for help (from God, from Our Lady, from the saints); seeking God's forgiveness and mercy when things go wrong (through prayer, and especially in the Sacrament of Confession). Sometimes we will be able to deepen our friendships with people in a chaste way, respecting our different commitments and relationships. At other times, we may need to let go of a certain relationship, because it is pulling us almost inevitably in a direction that is not good.

4. Sex outside marriage - Sex before or outside marriage is wrong: It means we are trying to share the intimacy and pleasure of married love without the total commitment or the openness to new life. And so love becomes distorted and damaged. This is obviously true of casual relationships, one-night-stands, and prostitution. But it is also true of relationships where there may be a deep love and friendship. Long-term relationships between a man and a woman, without the bond of marriage, do not have that lifelong commitment and stability that should be an essential part of sexual love and family life. And in same-sex relationships, even when there is a deep love and friendship between two people, there is not that fundamental openness to children that is an essential part of married love. It's not just that some same-sex couples happen to be unable to have children (many married couples are also unable to have children for various reasons); it is that these relationships by their very nature are closed to the possibility of new life. The 'complementarity' of man and woman which makes new life possible is part of the essential meaning of sex.

5. The need for love - In all these different cases, where sex is separated from marriage, the same core difficulties are present: a love that seeks the intimacy of sex without a lifelong commitment or an openness to new life. All of us who are not married, whatever reasons there are, whatever situations we are in, are called to live a chaste life and a life of sexual abstinence. It is good to remember two points: First, we should never judge or condemn anyone because of the way they feel or the way they understand their sexual orientation. It is our sexual behaviour that is at issue here, and the responsibility we all have to live chastely and to keep sex within the relationship of marriage. Second, this does not mean that all those who are not married are condemned to live lives without the fulfilment of love. We all need love, and there are many different ways that we are called to give and receive love - the love of friends, of family, of God, of fellow Christians, etc. But that very particular kind of love that is expressed in sexual intercourse is for those who are married, to bind a husband and wife together in a lifelong union and make them open to new life. This is not a human right, or even a fundamental human need - it is a gift and a vocation and a responsibility that comes to many people, but not to everyone.

DATING AND FRIENDSHIP

At the right time, in the right way, 'going out with someone' in an exclusive relationship can be a wonderful and important part of one's life, and even a preparation for an engagement and marriage. Here are some thoughts about dating.

1. Peer group pressure and dating - There is often a lot of pressure on people to be in a relationship. It can come from our peer group, or from society, and it makes us feel that life is empty and meaningless if we are not dating someone. This is not at all true! We certainly need love and friendship - but these can be found in many different relationships. Dating can be a chance to know someone better, to spend more time with them, to share their life - to see if we are right for each other. But it can also make a relationship narrow and even selfish; it can bind our hearts in a way that might not be good for us now; and cut us off from other friendships.

2. The freedom not to date - So don't assume that you have to be dating all the time, or that there is something wrong with you if you are single. If you are still young, or if you are not seriously considering marriage at this moment, then it is often better to stay single and put your time and emotional energy into strengthening friendships and getting to know new people. This gives your heart a kind of inner freedom to get stuck into other things; and it also means you have a bigger chance of meeting the right person when he or she comes along!

3. Friendship within a relationship - If you are dating, then of course you want to get to know the other person well and share your life with them. Friendship is the most important part of dating: Can you talk with each other, trust each other, forgive each other? Do you have things in common? Can you share your joys and sorrows, your strengths and weaknesses, your dreams and fears? Do you like who they are and what they care about? Do you respect and admire their principles, the way they treat people? Can you share what is closest to your heart - your hopes, your values, your faith? Ultimately, if you are considering marriage, the deepest question is not just: Do I love this person and do they love me? It is also: Are they a good person, a person of faith, who would be kind and loving and faithful - as a husband and father, as a wife and mother?

4. The risk of being exclusive - Two traps that couples often fall into, paradoxically, make it harder to know each other and grow in friendship. One is spending too much time together, in an exclusive way. A couple can get so focussed on each other and their relationship and their feelings, that they never see the other person in a bigger context: with other people, with other friends, with their own family members. You know someone partly through their relationships and their personal interests. So if you never see your boyfriend or girlfriend in other contexts or relationships, then it will be hard to know who they really are; and if they have no other interests than you, then perhaps they are not very interesting!

5. The risk of being too close, too quickly - The other trap is for a couple to become too close, emotionally or sexually. It is not just the lack of chastity, it is the fact that if we become too emotionally dependent or sexually involved, then we lose sight of the friendship. It's harder to see who the person really is, and what our relationship really means. We lose some of our freedom, and literally get trapped in our feelings or sexual needs. This lack of freedom is magnified if a couple live together before marriage. They are so involved, literally 'attached', that it becomes extra hard for them to see each other with clear eyes and a pure heart, and extra hard for them to step back and work out whether this is a truly good relationship.

HOW FAR CAN WE GO?

If you are dating, chastity is much more than 'not having sex'. But thinking about abstinence helps us to work out why we want to be chaste.

1. **Abstinence** - Sex is for marriage. It's as simple as that. In sex you give your whole self to another person: body, heart, mind, and soul; strengths and weaknesses; present and future; and your union makes the extraordinary gift of new life possible. If you do this without the lifelong commitment of marriage, or without being open to the gift of children, then you are distorting the very meaning of sex, and damaging the love that you share. So it is important to make a very

clear decision in your own mind that you will not sleep with your boyfriend or girlfriend, however close you are; and that you will keep your virginity until marriage. This is the meaning of abstinence. And if you have lost your virginity in the past, then go to confession, and really believe that you can make a new start and begin again. There is much more to chastity than just abstinence. But the decision not to have sex before marriage is a fundamental one that will bring you real joy and peace. It is a way of being faithful to your future husband or wife (because you are refusing to give your life in sexual love before marriage); it is a way of loving your present boyfriend or girlfriend and growing closer to them (because you are respecting the true nature of your relationship, which is one of friendship and affection); and it is a way of protecting your own purity of heart and freedom. Abstinence is one reason (but not the only one) why it is wrong for a couple to move in and live together before marriage.

2. General principles - So how far can we go? The real question is "Where are we going? What direction is this activity pulling me in?" If it is drawing my heart and body towards sexual intercourse, and leaving me frustrated and unfulfilled because I can't have sex, then it is not good for our relationship. A relationship of dating or engagement is meant to be about friendship, affection, trust, respect and love. Sexual feelings are bound to have a part in this; they are part of our humanity; and they can draw a couple closer together in a way that is good and holy - as long as they remain chaste and in a context of friendship and affection. But if something is making us lustful, then it is damaging the purity of that love, and it can be a temptation to sin. A couple needs to think and talk and pray about these questions, and to get advice from others that they trust. It is about discerning honestly what is happening in a relationship, what it means, and where it is leading. Growing in love together is a beautiful and complicated thing!

3. Practical advice - But a couple will rightly ask whether there are some guidelines about sexual intimacy - and there are. Some forms of intimacy are wrong because they arouse our hearts and bodies towards a longing for sexual intercourse, and they even become a kind of 'sexual intercourse' without the actual sex: mutual masturbation; undressing together; touching each other intimately; sharing a bed. Of course just looking at someone or holding hands can arouse passion! But that is different from doing something that we know pulls us in the direction of unchastity. So a simple and honest answer, which not everyone would agree with, but that seems to be wise: in the area of chastity, we should err on the side of caution: anything more than hugs and kisses is too far. And we need to be honest even about the hugs and kisses: are they a sign of true affection and friendship? Or are they making us lustful and leading us into temptation? If that is the case, then this is too far as well. Look at it this way: if you marry each other, you will never regret the times you have both been chaste and waited patiently during your time of dating and engagement. And if instead you split up sometime in the future, you will never regret preserving your purity with each other and keeping it for your future husband or wife.

4. Talking to each other about chastity - Are you able to talk about chastity and abstinence and your moral values with your boyfriend or girlfriend? Talking honestly, and having some common ground, are essential. The biggest issue is whether your boyfriend or girlfriend has the same desire to be chaste as you do, the same principles. If they do, then you can agree about how you hope to behave together, and you can try to live these things. If you don't have the same principles and hopes about chastity in your relationship, then it will be almost impossible to have a real understanding of what sort of relationship you are having. Even if they agree out of respect for you, it means you are both pulling in different directions. But whatever the case, you must talk

and agree what you want - it's no good improvising and
trying to keep the 'rules' in the heat of the moment.

**5. What if my boyfriend or girlfriend sees things
differently?** - If your boyfriend or girlfriend simply
can't respect your values, and is constantly pushing you
to go further than you want sexually, then it is probably
time to end the relationship. It means that as a couple
you have fundamental differences of outlook between
you, differences that will make love and marriage very
difficult; and it also means that this person has little
respect for your own values, or little self-control - either
of which should make your concerned. Chastity is a
beautiful thing, the greatest gift you can give to your
boyfriend or girlfriend, and to your future husband
or wife (whoever that will be). If you can make a
commitment to chastity and abstinence, and really believe
in their value, they will not be a burden; your heart
will feel liberated and joyful; and even the sacrifice of
resisting temptations can be a gift and bring peace.

- How to Discover your Vocation -

FIVE WAYS TO BECOME CLEARER
ABOUT YOUR VOCATION

The greatest vocation is simply to be a Christian, and this is given to us at our baptism. If we die young, or we don't discover a more specific Christian vocation, then we should not feel that we have wasted our life, or that our life is unfinished or unfulfilled. But many people are called to a more specific vocation as Christians: to marriage; to the priesthood; to the permanent diaconate; to 'consecrated life' as a monk or nun, as a religious brother or sister, or as a consecrated single person living in the world.

The normal way that God calls us to a particular vocation is through the deepest desires of our heart. So if we have had a deep and lasting desire to do one thing (e.g. to get married), and if we have never had a deep or lasting desire to do something else (e.g. to become a priest or religious brother or sister), then that is a fairly good indication that something is for us (in this case marriage).

It may be very clear to you which vocation you feel called to. If it is not, then here are some things you can do to help you become clearer, to help you listen to the Lord more and let him work in your life more. He will make things clear in his own good time - we can trust him.

1. Give your life to God! - Say to him, 'I am completely yours, I give you everything; I will do whatever you ask of me, I let go of all my fears and doubts. Show me your will, and I will follow it. I am yours'. Say this as a prayer, and really mean it. This is the only way we find true freedom; and only if we are free can he call us. He will not let you down; he won't ask you to do something that is wrong for you, or that you are unable to fulfil - all he wants is your willingness and openness.

2. Deepen your prayer life - Don't go mad, as if you can force God to give you an answer by praying all the time. But deepen your prayer life: have a routine, set aside some time each day, which includes at least some time each morning and evening. At the same time, deepen your love for the Mass. Don't rush it or waste it. Try and go to weekday Mass at least once a week as well as on Sunday, maybe more often if it is easy.

3. Grow in holiness - Be really honest with yourself about your faults and sins. Be really determined to live a life of holiness. Often the Lord can't speak to us, or we can't hear him, if we are not living a Christian life. If you are committed to your faith and discerning seriously, then try to go to confession every month, and stick at it - even if you feel you have nothing to say.

4. Nourish your spiritual life - There are two main ways we can do this. (i) *Find some good spiritual reading*. Have a book that you can dip into every day or two; something that inspires you about Christian faith or prayer or the lives of the saints. Read a little bit every day. Just make sure that it is spiritually nourishing for you, and that it is faithful, Catholic food. (ii) *Join a Catholic group*. It doesn't matter if it is a vocations discernment group, or a parish prayer group, or a Bible study group, or a young-adult socialising group. The main thing is to make sure that you are not living your faith alone, and that you have other people around to encourage you, and to help you see that you are not the only person exploring your direction in life.

5. Talk honestly with someone you trust - At some stage you need to talk about your sense of vocation and not just keep it to yourself. You might not find the ideal 'guru', but just try and think of someone who is wise and has a deep faith. It might be your parish priest, or another priest you know; it might be a wise layperson in the parish or somewhere else. You might call them your 'spiritual director', but the title is not important. It is good to have one-off conversations; but it is also good to have someone you can talk to over time, coming back to things; who can give advice and give an outside opinion; and can help you see some patterns in your faith and vocation that emerge over a period of time.

Gradually, you should find yourself becoming more attracted to one vocation, and less attracted to another. If you are really confused and stuck, and not sure which way to go, with contradicting signs and signals - then talk to someone, a priest or spiritual director. Get advice, get an outside opinion; don't get stuck in a rut. Above all: Don't be afraid. It is God who is leading you forward; he has plans for you, whatever they are; you can't go wrong if you are trying to do his will and listening and doing all you can. He won't let you down.

FIVE WAYS TO FIND A GOOD CATHOLIC
HUSBAND OR WIFE

Most young people hope to get married and have children one day. The clearest sign that marriage is for you is simply that have a desire to get married and have a family, and you do not have a sense of being pulled towards another vocation (see below about other vocations). If this is the case then it is perfectly reasonable to hope that you will be married, and to pray that God will help you to find a good husband or wife.

There are many happy and holy marriages between Catholics and non-Catholics, but if you are a Catholic it is a real blessing if you can find a husband or wife who shares your faith. This means that you will have the same Catholic values and the same understanding of the deepest meaning of marriage; that you can support each other in the practice of your own faith; and you can have a shared understanding of how to bring up your children in the Catholic faith. Here are some tips on finding such a husband or wife.

1. Pray every day that God will give you a good Catholic husband or wife - Just say a short, simple prayer for that intention every day; use your own words, or say a 'formal' pray for this intention such as the Our Father or Hail Mary. You can even do this if you are young and not thinking about marriage yet. And pray to the Virgin Mary and to St Joseph for this intention.

2. Find out more about the Catholic vision of marriage - Our ideas about marriage are formed by so many different influences: by our family background, by friends, by the media, etc. Some of our ideas will be good and healthy, but some of them might be distorted or just plain wrong. It will be a great help if we can find out more about the true Catholic vision of marriage - above all by reading (see some of the books in the "Relationships..." section at pp. 95-6 below). This vision will inspire us to seek a good Catholic husband or wife; it will help us to look for the right things in a relationship; and it will prepare us in a realistic way for the great challenge of married life.

3. Be a good person yourself - The best way to meet a good person, a person of faith, is to be a good person yourself, to be a person of faith. 'Like attracts like'. They are looking for someone full of love and goodness too. So live your faith. Live a life of prayer and love. Be the best person you can be. And this will help you to meet the right person and to build the best relationship you can.

4. Socialise with other Catholics - You don't have to socialise only with other Catholics. But if you want to meet a Catholic husband or wife, make sure you are actually meeting some other Catholics. Go to Catholic youth events, prayer groups, retreats, pilgrimages - anything at all! Use Facebook and other social networking websites to hook into Catholic groups and events in your area. If you feel comfortable with it, perhaps use a Catholic online dating website. You have to be cautious meeting people online, but it might be that you can discover a wider range of practicing Catholics on a Catholic website than you can in your ordinary social life.

5. Keep your relationship chaste while you are dating - A chaste relationship when you are dating is one of the clearest signs that a marriage will be happy and faithful. If you are having sex before marriage, or if you are getting sexually involved in a way that is too intimate before marriage, not only is this sinful, but it actually damages your relationship, and it makes it harder for you to understand and trust each other as boyfriend and girlfriend. Dating, and then engagement, are about growing in love and friendship, so that you are ready to make the commitment of marriage. The paradox is that people are less ready for marriage if they are already sexually involved. Living together is the worst possible preparation for marriage: it takes away your freedom to make a proper decision about the future; and it is no surprise that you are more likely to separate after marriage if you lived together before marriage. And if your boyfriend or girlfriend does not share your Catholic views about chastity before marriage, then he or she will probably not share your Catholic views about the true meaning of marriage itself.

FIVE 'SIGNS' OF A VOCATION TO THE PRIESTHOOD OR CONSECRATED LIFE

'Consecrated life' is the term used by the Church to mean all those people who have dedicated themselves to the Lord through life-long vows of poverty, chastity and obedience: monks and nuns who live in enclosed communities, brothers and sisters who live in community but are active in the world, and single men and women who have consecrated themselves in different ways. The term is used here to save time.

Below is a list of some of the ways that God can call people to priesthood or consecrated life. These are just some different things to look out for in your life. None of them, on its own, is final. Many of them also apply to lay people. It's the overall pattern that is important. If you keep coming back to a number of these things in the list below, then perhaps there is something there for you.

1. A desire to be a priest or consecrated person - Maybe you can't explain why you have this desire, it's a part of you, like falling in love. You just know that this is what seems right. You imagine yourself as a priest or consecrated person and it seems to fit, even if it makes you afraid or you think it would be impossible. There is a joy and excitement when you think about it, a sense that this is the right path. The idea keeps coming back. Some scripture passage or sermon seems to be directed at you - about the priesthood, or the call of the disciples, or service. There is a sense of being pulled or pushed in this direction. It might seem like something you are fighting against. You may find yourself making excuses to yourself (and even to others) about why you shouldn't become a priest or consecrated person, raising a list of objections.

2. An admiration for priests or consecrated people you know - You sense a goodness and holiness in their lives. You have an attraction to something they have or something they represent; even if you can't imagine being one. They seem to be living a life worth living, in a way that speaks to you. You are drawn to them. Or perhaps you do not have any explicit desires to be a priest or consecrated person, but you are attracted to many of the things that are involved in their lives. You have a desire to serve people in different ways, or to pass on the faith, or to pray with and for others. Maybe you find less satisfaction in your work, not because it is wrong, but you feel it is not enough.

3. An inner desire to pray more and to take the faith more seriously - You just find that you want to pray more and to deepen your faith. Your love for Christ is growing, and your love for the Church. More and more you desire to give your life to God completely. Of course this is true for many holy lay-people! But it can often be the beginning of a vocation to priesthood or consecrated life. You are not sure why, but you have a feeling that you can't hold anything back. For some people the idea of celibacy comes to mean more and more - not because they dislike marriage, but because they feel called to give their life wholeheartedly to serve God and others, in a way that would be difficult within the commitments of marriage and family life.

4. Other people affirm your vocation - When you talk to people about the possibility of priesthood or consecrated life, especially committed Catholics, they don't look as if you are mad. They affirm it, and say 'of course, I could have told you that years ago'. They encourage you. In other words, from the outside, this vocation also seems to make sense - it is not just a subjective sign for you, but it is beginning to be a more objective sign to others too. Perhaps people who don't know you even come up and suggest the priesthood or consecrated life to you, out of the blue! Perhaps there is someone wise and trustworthy that you have chatted to about your vocation over a period of time; you have talked things through with them and they know you quite well. If they affirm what you have said, and it seems to them that you may have a vocation, then this is another more public sign that it may be true.

5. A feeling that you are not worthy to be a priest or consecrated person - This might seem like a paradox, but it can be true. Sometimes someone may have a deep feeling that the priesthood or consecrated life is too much of an ideal for them, that they are not worthy, or not good enough, or not capable enough. These feelings can be a sign of humility, an indication that someone has a healthy sense of their own limitations, and a high sense of the dignity of this calling. The feeling of unworthiness may, strangely, be a sign that someone has a true appreciation for what this vocation means, and that they will be open to asking for God's help and the help of the Church.

If it seems to you that some of these signs are very clear and strong, or if many of them seem to come together and add up and begin to form a pattern, then this can be the clearest sign that the Lord is calling you at least to investigate and humbly take the next step. And if these signs are missing, or they are very weak in our lives, then the Lord is probably not calling us, at least not yet. Usually, God gives us enough to go on - he does not play games with us. We do not need to ask for 'supernatural' signs, visions, dreams, angels. We should certainly pray for help and guidance, but usually God will guide us in these ordinary ways.

If these signs grow stronger and come together, then we should take the next step - talk to someone we trust; talk to our parish priest, or the vocations director of the Diocese, or the vocations director of a religious order we are interested in. We move to a new stage in our discernment, which is trusting in the discernment of the Church, which is more objective and 'public' because it involves other people. At the end of the day, we can trust the Church to help us discern, and trust that the Lord is guiding us through the Diocese or community we are involved in.

- How to find Support and Information -

There are so many different books and websites and films that can help us in our faith. This selection is a slightly random list of things to get you started. The websites, of course, will change very quickly - so there is no guarantee that the content will still be good by the time you reach them!

You can order any of the books below from your local bookshop. Many are available much cheaper online in second-hand editions, for example at *www.amazon.com* or *www.abebooks.com*

BOOKS

Five essential books to buy and keep for a lifetime

The Bible: Make sure it is a complete Bible and not one with some of the 'books' left out. It should be a 'Catholic' Bible, or one with the deuterocanonical books of the Old Testament (called the Apocrypha by Protestants) included. Good modern translations include: The Ignatius Bible: Revised Standard Version, Catholic Edition, and The Ignatius Bible:Revised Standard Version, Second Catholic Edition. These Bibles can be obtained at *www.ignatius. com*. The CTS Catholic Bible has the scripture readings from Mass listed for easy reference.

The Catechism of the Catholic Church: Get the Revised Second Edition (which has a few improvements on the first). There are different editions published. This full catechism is actually a bit easier to read and understand than the shorter Compendium of the Catechism of the Catholic Church, which is often very dense.

The Sunday Missal: This contains the scripture readings and prayers for all the Sunday Masses of each year, and for some other big feasts. It means that we can look at the readings at home, and pray with them during the week. There are different versions of the Sunday Missal. The St Paul Sunday Missal is a cheaper paperback 'disposable' version that is reprinted each year with the correct readings and prayers just for that year.

A Simple Prayer Book (London: Catholic Truth Society): This contains all the traditional Catholic prayers; as well as the prayers of the Mass, Stations of the Cross, summary of Christian doctrine, etc. There are many other prayer books like this.

Butler's Lives of the Saints: There are many different versions of this book too, and in fact any good book which contains lives of the saints will help you.

Simple introductions to the Catholic Faith

Christianity: An Introduction to the Catholic Faith and *Living Life to the Full: An Introduction to the Moral and Social Teaching of the Catholic Church*, by David Albert Jones: (Oxford: Family Publications, 1999). [Two short pamphlets that form a pair. Clear and systematic explanations].

A Catechism of Christian Doctrine (London, Catholic Truth Society). [Traditional *'Penny Catechism'*, now updated, with famous succinct answers. E.g., Question 1: Who made you? Answer 1: God made me].

Catholic Christianity by Peter Kreeft (San Francisco: Ignatius Press, 2001). [A readable overview of the Catholic faith based on the Catechism. Available at *www. ignatius.com*.]

What is the Catholic Church? by Stephen Wang (London: Catholic Truth Society, 2007). [Small pamphlet which explains why it is important to belong to the Catholic Church].

YOUCAT: Youth Catechism of the Catholic Church. (San Francisco: Ignatius Press, 2010). [A popular, youth-inspired catechism of Catholic beliefs and practices. Available at *www.ignatius.com*.]

The How-To Book of Catholic Devotions by Aquilina and Flaherty (Our Sunday Visitor, 2000). [Step-by-step guidelines to the Church's devotions].

More in-depth works about the Catholic Faith

An Intelligent Person's Guide to Catholicism by Alban McCoy (London and New York: Continuum, 2001). [University talks about basic Catholic questions].

Letters to a Young Catholic by George Weigel (Leominster: Gracewing, 2004). [Full of stories and examples from Catholic lives].

Compendium of the Catechism of the Catholic Church (London: Catholic Truth Society, 2006): [Official shorter catechism of the Church in question and answer format. Quite dense and difficult in places].

Credo: The Catholic Faith Explained by Fr Marcus Holden and Fr Andrew Pinsent (London: CTS, 2007) [Beautifully illustrated pocket catechism].

The Teaching of Christ: A Catholic Catechism for Adults, 5th edition, edited by Donald W. Wuerl and Ronald Lawler: (Huntington, Indiana: Our Sunday Visitor, 2005). [Massive book. One of the best and most comprehensive catechisms; very clear. With references to the Catechism of the Catholic Church].

Spiritual classics

Often available in different translations and editions.

The Rule of St Benedict [How to be holy in community...].

The Imitation of Christ by Thomas a Kempis [How to know Christ and stay close to him...].

Introduction to the Devout Life by St Francis de Sales [How to be holy in ordinary life...].

Self-Abandonment to Divine Providence by Jean-Pierre De Caussade [How to find God in the present moment...].

Story of a Soul by St Thérèse of Lisieux [How to love in the little things...].

The Screwtape Letters by C.S. Lewis [Spiritual advice in reverse: a senior devil explains to his junior how to trap and bring down a new Christian].

Something Beautiful for God: Mother Teresa of Calcutta by Malcolm Muggeridge (HarperCollins 1997). [An early biography that brought Mother Teresa to the attention of the world].

Practical advice

Seventeen Steps to Heaven: A Catholic Guide to Salvation by Leo J. Trese (Sophia, 2001). [Practical steps which will help you to live your faith more fully].

Gangster's Guide to God by John Pridmore and Greg Watts (xt3 Media, 2007). [Honest, practical advice about all aspects of the Christian life - especially for young people].

Catholic Student Guide: Essential Reading for Life at University, 2nd Edition, edited by Peter Kahn (Family Publications, 2006). [Written by chaplains and students themselves, covering gap years, accommodation, student lifestyle and study, Catholic chaplaincies and times of Mass].

Relationships, Chastity, and Dating

Pure Love by Jason Evert (San Diego: Catholic Answers, 2007). [Excellent pamphlet about love, chastity, dating, sex, etc].

If You Really Loved Me: 100 Questions on Dating, Relationships, and Sexual Purity by Jason Evert (Cincinnati: St Anthony Messenger, 2003).

Real Love: Answers Your Questions on Dating, Marriage and the Real Meaning of Sex by Mary Beth Bonacci (San Francisco, Ignatius Press, Rev. 2012).

We're on a Mission from God by Mary Beth Bonacci (San Francisco: Ignatius Press, 1996).

The Catholic Family Handbook by Lawrence G. Lovasik (Manchester, NH: Sophia, 2000). ["Time-Tested Techniques to Help You Strengthen Your Marriage and Raise Good Kids"].

WEBSITES

Learning about the Catholic Faith

Catholic Answers: *www.catholic.com* Questions, answers, articles, reports, forums, etc - about all aspects of Catholic belief and practice.

xt3: *www.xt3.com* "The number 1 global youth community". Articles, links, videos, chat, forums.
EWTN: *www.ewtn.com* Online TV, radio, Catholic resources etc.

Peter Kreeft: *www.peterkreeft.com* Catholic writer and speaker. Many articles and audio talks.

Godspy: *www.godspy.com* Online magazine for Catholics and seekers.

Life Teen: http://lifeteen.com/. Online version of the Catholic youth outreach effort.

Catholic Underground. Go to: catholicunderground.net/home.html.

CaFE - Catholic Faith Exploration: *www.catholicevangel.org* Modern media resources. A great selection of DVDs, audio CDs, etc, for personal or group use; on topics such as knowing God, the Catholic Church, the Mass, growing in faith, scripture and social action.

Prayer

www.scborromeo.org/prayers.htm A great list of prayers and devotions.

www.catholic-pages.com/DIR/prayers.asp Loads of articles about prayer.

www.scborromeo.org/ccc.htm Christian prayer as explained in the Catechism.

Sacred Space: www.sacredspace.ie Guided meditation on the web.

Pray As You Go: www.pray-as-you-go.org Music readings, meditation, etc as podcasts.

Relationships, Chastity, and Dating

www.chastity.com The 'Chastity Q&A' section is full of practical advice.

www.lovematters.com "Dating, sex, love, and you - how to survive and find true love…"

Vocation

United States Conference of Catholic Bishops Vocations: www.usccb.org/beliefs-and-teachings/vocations/. Source for information from US bishops of vocations to ordained ministry and consecrated life.

Vocation Boom: www.vocationboom.com. Vocation Boom is a non-profit effort to help promote priestly vocations.

Institute on Religious Life: http://www.religiouslife.com/. This organization promotes discernment of vocations to religious life.

FILMS

There are so many inspirational films to watch on DVD. Here are a few Bible stories:

The Passion of the Christ: Mel Gibson's emotional and harrowing epic. Available from Ignatius Press: *www. ignatius.com.*

The Greatest Story Ever Told: Inspiring grand-scale recreation of the Life of Jesus.

Jesus of Nazareth: A TV mini series by Zeffirelli. Available from Ignatius Press: *www.ignatius.com.*

The Prince of Egypt: Moses Animation.

The Miracle Maker: Jesus Animation.

The Nativity Story: Thoroughly researched with spectacular recreation of historical settings - from Mary's perspective. Available from Ignatius Press: *www.ignatius.com.*

And some other great films

Clare and Francis: A film about St. Clare and St. Francis of Assisi, available from Ignatius Press, *www.ignatius.com.*

A Man For All Seasons: The life of English martyr St Thomas More - lawyer, politician, husband, father. Six academy awards. Available from Ignatius Press: *www. ignatius.com.*

Edith Stein: A dramatic account of the Jewish convert to the Catholic faith, philosopher, Carmelite sister, and martyr, who gave her life at Aucshwitz. Available from Ignatius Press: *www.ignatius.com*.

The Song of Bernadette: Classic 1943 film about Lourdes and the life of St Bernadette. Available from Ignatius Press: *www.ignatius.com*.

Cosmic Origins. An outstanding film showing how science points to God. Available from Ignatius Press: *www.ignatius.com*.

Bernadette. A contemporary retelling of the true-story of St. Bernadette and the visions of Our Lady of Lourdes. Stars Sydney Penny. Available from Ignatius Press: *www. ignatius.com*.

Karol: A Man Who Became Pope: A powerful full-length feature film charting the early life of Pope John Paul II. Available from Ignatius Press: *www.ignatius.com*.

Fishers of Men: American Bishops' Vocational Promotion, 2006. "No movie has come close to portraying the beauty of the priesthood in such a powerful way". (Search for online version).

For a wonderful selection of Catholic DVDs, audio talks etc, see...

Ignatius Press: www.ignatius.com.

Higher Education Chaplaincies

For information about student chaplaincies at colleges and universities, see:

FOCUS-the Fellowship of Catholic University Students. Online at http://www.focus.org.

Other Groups and Communities
that might interest young people

Cenacolo Community: www.comunitacenacolo. it (communities for those suffering from addictions, especially to drugs, living a simple lifestyle of work, prayer, and spiritual healing).

Community of St John: www.stjean.com (French monastic community, male and female branches in UK).

Cursillo: www.cursillo.org.uk (courses for Christian renewal).

Emmanuel Community: www.emmanuelcommunity.com (charismatic inspired mainly lay community).

Focolare: www.focolare.org.uk and *www.focolare.org* (founded by Chiara Lubich; members meet in small groups to share experiences of living the Gospel and support each other; youth events).

Franciscan Friars of the Renewal (CFR): *www. franciscanfriars.com* (live simply and work with the poor and in youth evangelisation).

L'Arche: *www.larche.org.uk* (Communities for people with and without learning difficulties and disabilities to live together).

Maltfriscans: *www.maltfriscans.org* (charismatic Franciscan/Carmelite movement; music and evangelisation).

Neo-Catechumenal Way: *www.camminoneocatecumenale .it/new/* (evangelisation and formation; parish-based communities centred on the Eucharist and the Word of God).

Opus Dei: *www.opusdei.org.uk* (talks, retreats, pastoral care etc; helps people to grow closer to God through their work and daily activities).

Verbum Dei: *www.fmverbumdei.com* [Spanish site] (preaching, teaching, giving retreats based on Scripture; *lectio divina*; helping in parishes).

FORMED®
THE CATHOLIC FAITH. ON DEMAND.

Discover the site that gathers more Catholic content in one place.

One convenient website

Save the time you used to s
searching and find the Cath
content you want. On dema
and available when you are.

High quality

You'll always
find beautiful,
trustworthy,
Catholic content.

New and updated regularly

Discover new
fresh materia
every week.

More choices

Easily choose from a wide range of
content options: movies, Ebooks,
audio talks, and video studies.

Login to formed.org for a free 7-day trial.